YOU SHOULD MEET

Duke Kahanamoku

by Laurie Calkhoven
illustrated by Stevie Lewis

Ready-to-Read

Simon Spotlight
New York   London   Toronto   Sydney   New Delhi

SIMON SPOTLIGHT

An imprint of Simon & Schuster Children's Publishing Division

1230 Avenue of the Americas, New York, New York 10020

This Simon Spotlight edition May 2017

Text copyright © 2017 by Simon & Schuster, Inc.

Illustrations copyright © 2017 by Stevie Lewis

SIMON SPOTLIGHT, READY-TO-READ, and colophon are registered trademarks of Simon & Schuster, Inc.

For information about special discounts for bulk purchases, please contact Simon & Schuster

Special Sales at 1-866-506-1949 or business@simonandschuster.com.

Manufactured in the United States of America 0521 LAK

4 6 8 10 9 7 5

Cataloging-in-Publication Data for this title is available from the Library of Congress.

ISBN 978-1-4814-9701-5 (hc)

ISBN 978-1-4814-9700-8 (pbk)

ISBN 978-1-4814-9702-2 (eBook)

CONTENTS

Introduction

Have you ever wondered what it would be like to live right next to the ocean? To ride ocean waves on a surfboard? Or to bring home an Olympic gold medal? Or several gold medals?

If so, then you should meet Duke Kahanamoku (ka-HA-na-mo-koo). Duke grew up on the beach in Hawaii. The ocean was his playground. He took part in four Olympics and created world swimming records. Then he showed the world how to surf ocean waves as tall as skyscrapers.

Duke brought *aloha*, or love, peace, and kindness, to the world. Once you meet him, you'll be inspired to do the same.

Chapter 1
Growing Up on the Beach

Duke Kahanamoku was born in Hawaii on August 24, 1890. His father was a police officer, and his mother was active in the community. Duke was their first child. Eventually, he would have eight siblings.

Hawaii wasn't the popular vacation spot that it is now. There were no big hotels, just the ocean and beautiful beaches.

When he was four, Duke's father and uncle taught him to swim "the Hawaiian way." They threw him over the side of a canoe, ready to jump in right away if he needed them. Duke didn't. He swam!

As a boy, Duke spent most of his time at the beach. He swam, paddled canoes, and took part in an ancient Hawaiian sport:

surfing. Duke, like other Hawaiians, called it wave riding.

He also sold newspapers, delivered ice, and showed tourists around to earn money for his family. Other days he went fishing to provide food. In school he played sports like football and soccer, but in his mind nothing could compete with surfing and swimming.

Duke was such a good swimmer that when the Amateur Athletic Union (AAU) had a race in Hawaii in 1911, he entered. (The AAU is one of the largest, nonprofit, volunteer, sports organizations in the United States. The AAU is dedicated to the development of amateur sports and physical fitness programs.) Hawaii didn't have an Olympic-size swimming pool, so they held the race in Honolulu Harbor.

Duke smashed the world record for the hundred-yard freestyle race by more than four seconds. Then he broke the American fifty-yard freestyle record by more than a second. A second may not seem like much time to you, but one second is an extremely long and important amount of time in Olympic sports. A person can win a gold medal at the Olympics by beating their opponent by only *one-tenth* of a second!

It was time for the world to learn the name of this Hawaiian swimmer!

Chapter 2
Olympic Dreams

The AAU didn't believe that a surfer they had never heard of could swim that fast. They said that officials must have timed the race incorrectly by using alarm clocks instead of stopwatches. They hadn't. Then the AAU decided the ocean currents helped Duke. He didn't get credit for breaking the records.

Duke's friends knew that he was the best swimmer in the world. They took up a collection to send him to the mainland to try out for the Olympics.

Duke boarded a ship to California. Then he rode trains across the country. He saw snow for the first time in the Rocky Mountains. In Chicago in February he had to buy warm clothes and a coat. He also swam in a pool for the first time.

At first Duke didn't like swimming in pools. The water was colder than Hawaii's tropical waters. He also had never learned how to turn when he hit a wall to swim laps and finish a race. But Duke didn't give up. Coaches helped him, and he began to win races. Soon he had a spot on the 1912 United States Olympic team. He was going to Sweden!

On June 14, 1912, the SS *Finland* set sail for Sweden with the Olympic team on board. Every ship, ferry, and tugboat in the New York harbor blew their foghorns at full blast to cheer on the athletes.

On the ship, Duke made many friends. He had his ukulele with him, and at night he played and sang Hawaiian songs. He trained the best he could in the ship's small canvas swimming tanks.

In Sweden, Duke became a sensation for his fast swimming. But he almost missed an important race. Duke's family always teased him because he could sleep anywhere, anytime. That was true even at the Olympics.

When it was time for the hundred-meter finals, Duke was nowhere to be found. His teammates rushed around searching for him. Finally, they found him taking a nap under a bridge! When they woke him up, he apologized and then went on to win the race.

Duke went on to win the final race too. He matched the world record on top of winning the gold medal.

Later that week Duke participated in the 4 x 200 meter relay, and the US team won the silver medal. He became one of the most famous swimmers in the world.

Chapter 3
The Human Fish

After the Olympics, everyone wanted to know more about the man nicknamed "the Human Fish." For the next few months, Duke traveled around the United States giving swimming demonstrations. He also surfed.

Surfing was known in California and Hawaii. But most people on the East Coast had never seen it done—that is, until Duke visited Atlantic City. He took to the waves, riding his board backward, standing on his head, and even carrying a boy on his shoulders. People went crazy for surfing and for Duke.

It wasn't until October 1912 that Duke was able to make his way back to Hawaii.

Duke waved his hat from the ship's deck. Then he dipped two fingers and raised them to his mouth. He wanted to let the crowd know that he couldn't wait to eat his favorite Hawaiian food again: *poi*. (Poi is a Hawaiian food made from taro root that is cooked, pounded, and molded into a paste. It is served in small bowls, and Hawaiians eat it by dipping two fingers in the bowl.) Duke's welcome-home party lasted an entire week!

Hawaii's most famous citizen settled back into day-to-day life. He kept swimming and surfing.

When World War I broke out in Europe in 1914, Duke raised money for the Red Cross and taught people about water safety and lifesaving. Then he traveled to Australia. People wanted to see him swim, but one look at the ocean reminded Duke of his happy days surfing in Hawaii. He wanted to surf again.

He made his own surfboard and took to the waters outside of Sydney. Once again, he was a surfing sensation. Before he left, he showed the Australians how to make surfboards. Pretty soon, surfing was one of Australia's most popular sports.

Surfing became even more popular at home when Duke rode a wave in 1917 that surfers still talk about today. The massive waves that day may have been caused by an earthquake in the middle of the Pacific Ocean. Duke only knew that the waves off the coast of Waikiki in Hawaii were the largest he'd ever seen.

He paddled far out into the water and waited for the tallest, fastest wave of them all.

When it came, Duke paddled hard. At the right time, he stood on his board. Then Duke rode that fast wave for more than a mile.

"I never caught another wave anything like that one," he later said, "It is a golden

Chapter 4
Hero

Duke hoped that surfing would become an Olympic sport. It never did, so he continued to compete as a swimmer. The 1916 Olympics were canceled because of World War I. Duke swam for the 1920 United States Olympic team in Antwerp, Belgium, and won gold in the hundred-meter freestyle on his thirtieth birthday. He also broke his own world record. Then he won the gold as part of the 4 x 200 freestyle relay team.

In the 1924 Olympics in Paris, France, eight swimmers from around the world were in the hundred-meter freestyle final. American swimmer Johnny Weissmuller found himself between Duke on one side and Duke's younger brother Sam on the other.

Duke wished both Johnny and Sam luck. "The most important thing in this race is to get the American flag up there three times," he said. "Let's do it."

The starting gun went off, and the swimmers dove into the pool. Johnny took the gold. Duke won the silver. And Sam won the bronze medal.

A bad case of the flu kept Duke from training for the 1928 Olympics. He didn't qualify for the team. He returned to the Olympics in Los Angeles, California, in 1932 as an alternate with the water polo team. All together, he took part in four Olympics! By the time Duke's Olympic career was over in 1932, he had won three gold medals and two silver.

Duke also gained fame for other reasons. In between the Olympic

Games, he acted in more than two dozen Hollywood movies.

Because of the color of his skin, Duke was only hired for small parts like pirates, servants, and Native American chiefs. When restaurants refused to serve him, Duke knew he was being treated unfairly, but he was a peaceful person and kept quiet. But he always knew in his heart these people were wrong to judge him by the color of his skin.

On June 14, 1925, Duke became a hero for another reason. He was relaxing on the beach in California with a couple of friends. They saw a fishing boat, the *Thelma*, in trouble off the coast. A storm had come up suddenly, and the boat was struggling in massive waves.

The boat capsized. All the fishermen on board fell into the ocean.

Duke didn't think twice. He grabbed his surfboard and dove into the pounding waves.

"I paddled until my arms begged for mercy," he later said.

Duke grabbed three men, pulled them onto his surfboard, and raced back to shore. Then he turned around and did it again, and again. He would have gone back a fourth time, but by then it was too late. A few of the men had already drowned.

Duke saved eight fishermen that day. His friends saved another four. But Duke didn't feel like the hero the world said he was. He was sad that some men had died before he got to them.

Today, largely because of Duke's
actions, lifeguards have rescue boards.

At the time, the police chief said
that Duke's actions were "the most
superhuman rescue act and the finest
display of surfboard riding that has ever
been seen in the world."

Chapter 5
The Ambassador of Aloha

Hawaii was always Duke's favorite place to be. When his Olympic career was over, he left Hollywood to settle down at home. He took different jobs and spent as much time on the beach as he could. Then he ran for sheriff of Honolulu and won. He also fell in love and got married at the age of fifty. He and his wife had no children.

Duke was sheriff from 1934 to 1961. After Hawaii became a state in 1959, he became Hawaii's Ambassador of Aloha. He welcomed guests to the islands and surfed.

Duke welcomed athletes like Babe Ruth and world figures like England's Queen Mother to Hawaii. Duke taught the Queen Mother how to do the hula! Even President John F. Kennedy wanted to meet the Human Fish!

Duke continued to be Hawaii's most famous citizen until Barack Obama was elected president in 2008.

Called the "father of modern surfing," Duke won many honors. You can find Duke's name in the US Olympic Hall of Fame. In 1999, *Surfer* magazine named him the "Surfer of the Century." He even got his own postage stamp from the United States Postal Service.

You'll find statues
of Duke on Freshwater Beach in
Australia and on the beach
at Waikiki, Hawaii.

But what mattered most to
Duke was bringing surfing and the
spirit of Hawaii to the rest of the world.

Duke's statue on the beach at Waikiki, in Hawaii. People like to leave flower necklaces, (called *leis*) on its arms as a tribute to Duke.

When Duke was a boy, only a few native Hawaiians still surfed. Thanks in large part to him, today surfing is a pastime enjoyed by people all over the world. It's an important part of the legacy of the Hawaiian people, a favorite sport, and a tool used by lifeguards to save lives.

Duke had this thought printed on the back of his business card. "In Hawaii we greet friends, loved ones, and strangers with Aloha, which means with love," he wrote. "Try meeting or leaving people with Aloha. You'll be surprised by their reaction."

BUT WAIT...

THERE'S MORE!

Now that you've read about Duke Kahanamoku, turn the page to learn to speak a few Hawaiian phrases, read about the history of Hawaii, and quiz yourself to see how much you've learned!

Speak Hawaiian!

Did you know that the Hawaiian language was almost lost? After British explorers, other Europeans, and Americans arrived in Hawaii, children were forced to speak English in school. By the early 1980s, there were approximately two thousand Hawaiian natives who spoke the language fluently. But the language is back on the rise. Now there are more than eighteen thousand Hawaiian speakers. Learn a few phrases from the Aloha State!

A quick conversation

Hello (also, "good-bye" and "love"): *Aloha* [say: ah-LOW-ha]

How are you?: *Pehea ʻoe?* [say: pay-HAY-ah OH-ay]

Same as usual: *ʻO ia mau nō* [say: oh ya maw noh]

I am fine: *Maikaʻi no au* [say: MY-kah ee NEW-ow]

Until we meet again: *A hui hou* [say: ah-HOO-ee-how]

Good-bye: *Aloha* [say: ah-LOW-ha]

Mind your manners!

Welcome! Enter!: *E komo mai* [say: eh KOH-moh MAH-ee]

Please: *E ʻoluʻolu* [say: eh oh-LOO oh-LOO]

Thank you: *Mahalo* [say: mah-HA-low]

You're welcome/No problem: *ʻAʻole pilikia*
[say: ah-OH-lay pee-lee-KEE-ah]

Who is that?

Family, relative: *'Ohana* [say: oh-HA-nah]

Parent: *Makua* [say: mah-KOO-ah]

Grandparent: *Kapuna* [say: Kah-POO-nah]

Teacher: *Kumu* [say: KOO-moo]

Child: *Keiki* [say: kay-EE-kee]

Friend: *Hoaloha* [say: HO-ah-low-ha]

What is that?

Wave: *Nalu* [say: NAH-loo]

Sky: *Lani* [say: LAH-nee]

Moon: *Mahina* [say: mah-HEE-nah]

Coconut: *Niu* [say: NEE-oo]

Shark: *Manō* [say: mah-NO]

When in Hawaii!

Good luck: *Pōmaika'i* [say: po-MY-kah-ee]

Happy New Year: *Hau'oli Makahiki Hou*
[say: ha-OH-lee MAH-kah-ee-kee ho]

Snacks or appetizers: *Pūpū* [say: poo-poo]

Love and care for the land: *Aloha 'āina*
[say: ah-LOW-ha AYN-eh]

Triggerfish (Hawaii's state fish):
Humuhumunukunukuapua'a [say: hoo-moo-
hoo-moo-noo-koo-noo-koo-ah-POO-ah-ah]

History of Hawaii

Hawaii is a string of islands in the Pacific Ocean. It is almost as far from California as New York is! So how did these tropical islands become one of the fifty United States of America? The first people who settled around 400 CE in the Hawaiian Islands traveled more than two thousand miles by canoe from other islands in the Pacific. They developed a language and culture, and for fun, they surfed! In 1810 King Kamehameha united the small, independent islands and established the Hawaiian monarchy. He is still celebrated every year on Kamehameha Day.

When the king died in 1819, everything changed. People came from other parts of the world, bringing their religions, languages, cultures, and germs. Tens of thousands of Hawaiians died from American and European diseases. Meanwhile, foreign businessmen bought up land for sugarcane plantations. By the end of the century, the few surviving Hawaiians found themselves in a kingdom controlled by American companies.

Queen Liliuokalani, the last Hawaiian ruler, fought to preserve Hawaiian independence but was overpowered by the businessmen. With the help of the US military, she was dethroned in 1893 and put under house arrest in 1895. She spent the rest of her life writing songs and poems about her home, including "Aloha Oe," Hawaii's signature song.

The president of the newly formed Republic of Hawaii eventually handed the country over to the United States in 1898. The Territory of Hawaii was an organized incorporated territory of the United States that existed from 1898 until August 21, 1959, when Hawaii became a state. The citizens now have a voice in the future of Hawaii and in the future of the United States. Thanks to efforts made by today's citizens, the Hawaiian culture is alive and flourishing.

45

Hawaiian Culture

The Hula

You might have seen a postcard or video of a group of people dancing the *hula* (say: HOO-la) at a *luau* (say: LOO-ow). Dancers often wear garlands of flowers around their shoulders, heads, wrists, and ankles. There is more to these beautiful dances than meets the eye. The two main types of this dance are hula *'auana* (say: ah-WAN-na), which is modern hula, and *kahiko* (say: kah-HEE-koh),

which is ancient. The hula *kahiko* often tells a story of gods and goddesses,

battles, and other traditional stories. The hula *'auana* incorporates instruments like ukulele, guitar, steel guitar, and bass. The hula dance accompanies a *mele* (say: MAY-lay), which is a song. The *mele* can tell any story that celebrates the spirit of Hawaii.

The Lei

A *lei* [say: lay] is a garland of flowers, leaves, shells, feathers, or other natural materials worn around the shoulders. It arrived in Hawaii with the Polynesian people in 400 or 500 CE. Over time, Hawaiians developed many different kinds of lei. They are made from different materials, carry various meanings, and are used for many occasions.

It is believed that a person puts a bit of themselves into each lei that he or she makes. For that reason, it is rude to refuse a lei or take one off in front of the person who gave it to you.

Lei made of the green *maile* (say: MY-lay) plant were once used to symbolize peace after a battle. Now they are worn at weddings, graduations, and other special celebrations. Maile is associated with the goddess of hula.

Lehua (say: lay-HOO-ah) leis are made from the bright red flowers and leaves of the lehua tree. The volcano goddess Pele is said to prize these flowers. They are placed as offerings to her at the crater of volcanoes.

Royal leis are made of stronger natural materials like shell, bone, feathers, nuts, and animal teeth. They are worn by kings, queens, and other powerful and respected people in the community.

Because they are made of flowers and other natural materials, most leis are not made to last. Traditionally, they are buried, hung on a tree branch, or thrown into the ocean once they are no longer being worn.

Poi

Poi (say: poy) is a traditional Hawaiian dish dating back as far as the Polynesian settlers. It is made from the root of the taro plant. It is pounded into a thick paste. Then it is left to ferment, or sour.

Traditionally, poi is eaten with the hands out of a bowl. Nowadays, the taro plant is used to make much more than poi. It can be found in smoothies, hummus, chips, and more!

Now that you've met Duke, what have you learned?

1. What year was Duke born?

a. 1890 b. 1959 c. 1776

2. Duke learned to swim "the Hawaiian way." What's another way to say that?

a. on land b. swimming upstream c. sink or swim

3. In Duke's first official swim competition in 1911, how did he do in the hundred-yard freestyle?

a. He tied for first place. b. He finished in record time. c. He lost.

4. Where were the Olympics held in 1912?

a. Chicago b. Sweden c. California

5. What nickname did Duke earn at the 1912 Olympics?

a. Father of Modern Surfing b. Dependable Duke c. the Human Fish

6. What did Duke do after the Olympics?

a. traveled Sweden b. traveled the United States c. went straight home

7. What did Duke teach the Australians to do?

a. make surfboards b. swim the butterfly c. make poi

8. What did the police chief call the "finest display of surfboard riding"?

a. breaking a world record b. winning a gold medal c. the *Thelma* rescue

9. What was Duke's title when he met John F. Kennedy?

a. lifeguard b. member of the US Olympic team

c. Ambassador of Aloha

10. On his business cards, how did Duke suggest we meet and leave people?

a. with love b. with surprise c. with gifts

Answers: 1. a 2. c 3. b 4. b 5. c 6. b 7. a 8. c 9. c 10. a